Alfred's Basic Piano Library

Piano

Fun Book · Level 3

D1540706

A COLLECTION OF 17 ENTERTAINING SOLOS

At the Carnival 6
Big Chief Yellow Hand 26
Calypso Rhumba 20
Carousel Waltz, The 14
Chromatic Rag 10
Concert Piece 30
Festive Dance 28
Jazz Sequences 8
Modern Sounds 18
Oh Where, Oh Where? 16
Pop! Goes the Weasel 32
Song for a Rainy Day 17
Spooky Story, A 22
Turkey in the Straw 4
Waltz in A Minor 24
Western Skies 2
White Coral Bells 12

FUN BOOK 3 of Alfred's Basic Piano Library contains 17 short pieces, carefully coordinated PAGE BY PAGE with the material in LESSON BOOK 3. These selections may be used *in addition to* or *instead of* the pieces in RECITAL BOOK 3, to provide additional reinforcement to the concepts emphasized in each piece. They may also be used as extra material for sight reading. However they are used, they should serve to make the course more flexible and more easily adaptable to the taste and needs of the individual student.

This book also answers the often expressed need for a variety of supplementary material for use when two or more students from the same family are studying from the same course and prefer not to play exactly the same pieces.

The subjects for the selections composed especially for this book were often suggested by students and teachers, with a view to adding good humor and amusement to the lesson. It is our hope that this book will live up to its name, for teachers and students alike.

The Authors

 A General MIDI disk is available (8565) which includes a full piano recording and background accompaniment.

Western Skies

Use after ON TOP OF OLD SMOKY, LESSON BOOK 3, (page 4).

Lazily and quietly

2nd time 8va

EXTENDED POSITION

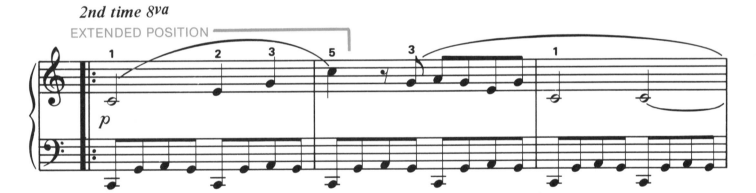

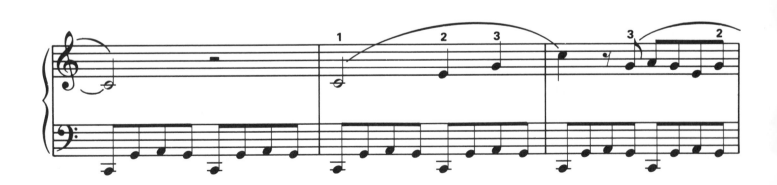

*You may play the pairs of eighth notes a bit unevenly, long short, long short, etc. in "WESTERN STYLE," if you wish.

Turkey in the Straw

Use after ALPINE MELODY (page 8).

KEY OF D MAJOR
Key Signature: 2 sharps (F# & C#)

Allegro Moderato

Folk Tune

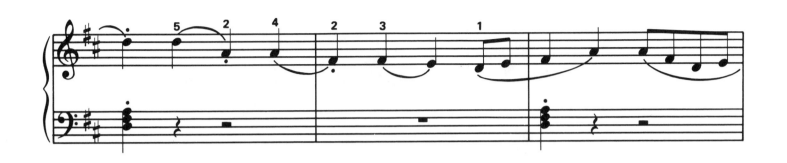

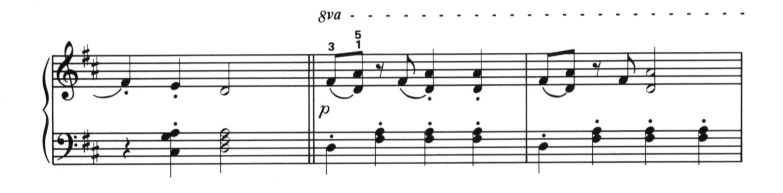

At the Carnival

Use after WALTZ PANTOMIME (page 10).

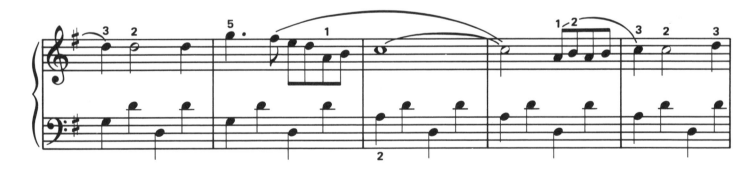

*Go back to the beginning, play to the sign ⊕; then play the Coda.

Jazz Sequences*

Use after ROMAN HOLIDAY (page 14).

Allegro Moderato

2nd time both hands 8va

*The repetition of a musical pattern, beginning on a higher or lower note, is called a *sequence*.

D.C. al ⊕, then play CODA

CODA

Both hands 8va - ¬ loco (as written)

Chromatic Rag

Use after VILLAGE DANCE (page 19).

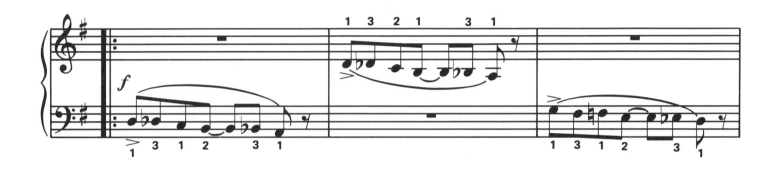

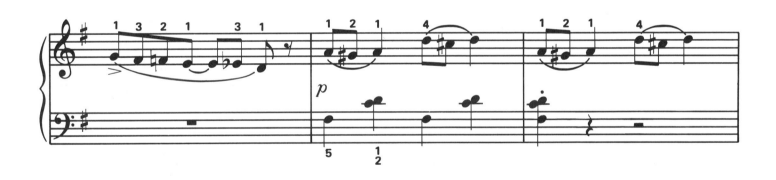

D.C. al Fine

White Coral Bells

Use after CASEY JONES (page 21).

KEY OF F MAJOR
Key Signature: 1 flat (B♭)

Moderately slow

English Round Melody

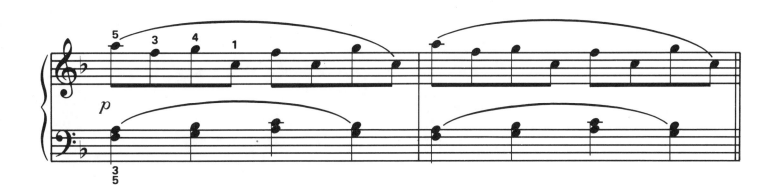

Oh,   don't you   wish   that   you could hear them   ring?

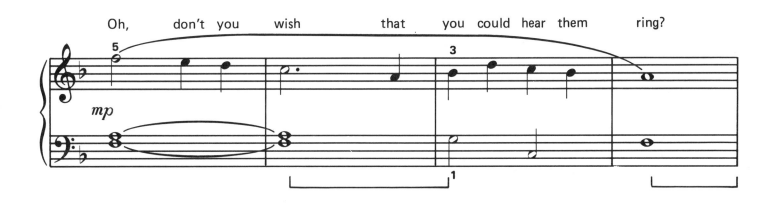

That will hap-pen   on-ly when the   wee   folk   sing.

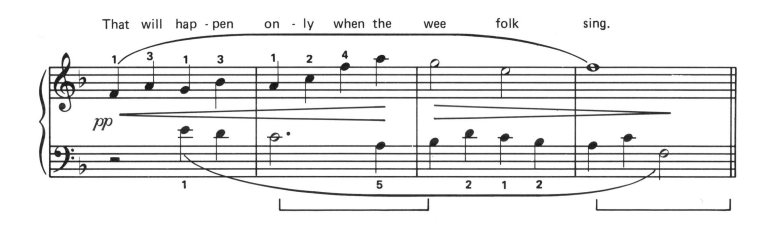

Both hands 2 octaves higher

ritardando

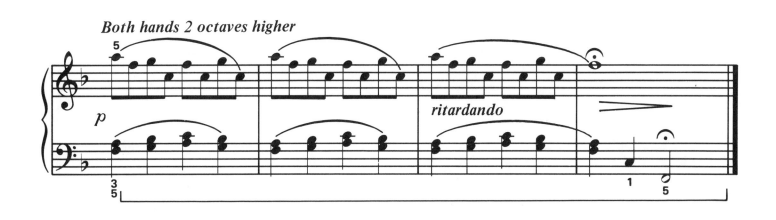

14

The Carousel Waltz

Use after A DAY IN VIENNA (page 22).

KEY OF F MAJOR
Key Signature: 1 flat (B♭)

Allegro moderato

Fine

*Play the F and G together with the side tip of the thumb.

Oh Where, Oh Where?

Use after A DAY IN VIENNA (page 22).

KEY OF F MAJOR
Key Signature: 1 flat (B♭)

Allegro moderato

Traditional

2nd time, play L.H. one octave lower

Song for a Rainy Day

Use after ENCHANTED CITY (page 25).

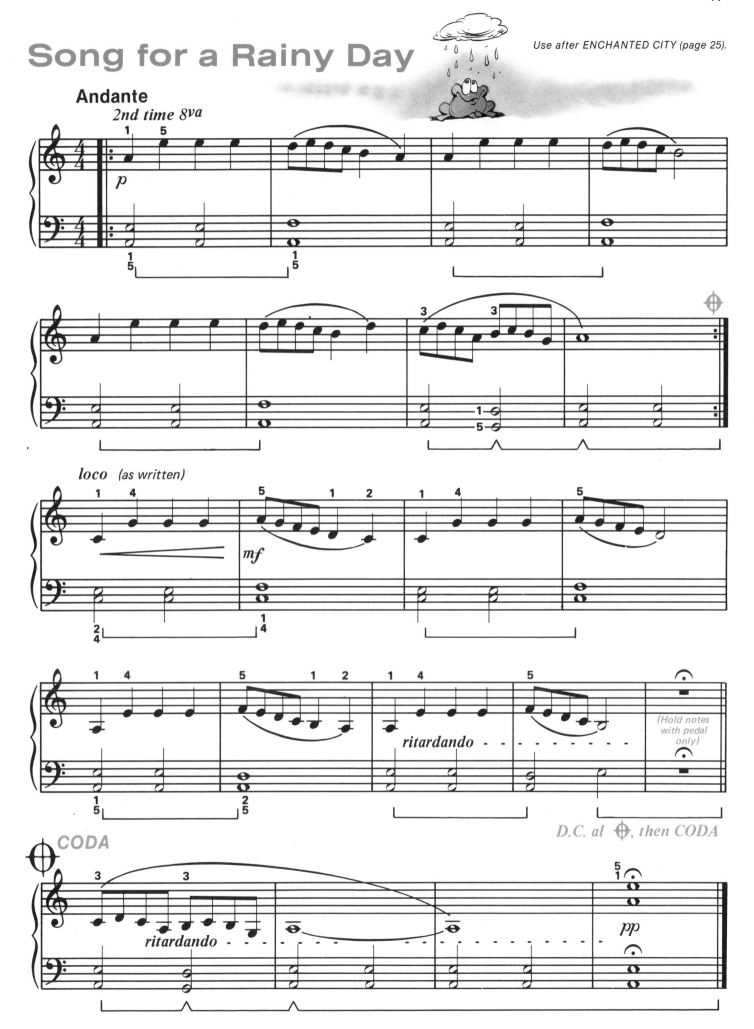

Modern Sounds

Use after MAKE UP YOUR MIND (page 27).

This piece begins with the R.H. and L.H. moving up and down the keyboard in thirds. All the thirds are fingered with the 2nd and 4th fingers. R.H. and L.H. 2's are on neighboring white keys.

In the 2nd section only the R.H. plays thirds. The L.H. plays fifths with 5 and 1.

This piece shows how thirds and fifths can be used to produce very modern sounds.

STARTING POSITION

KEY OF C MAJOR
Key Signature: no ♯, no ♭.

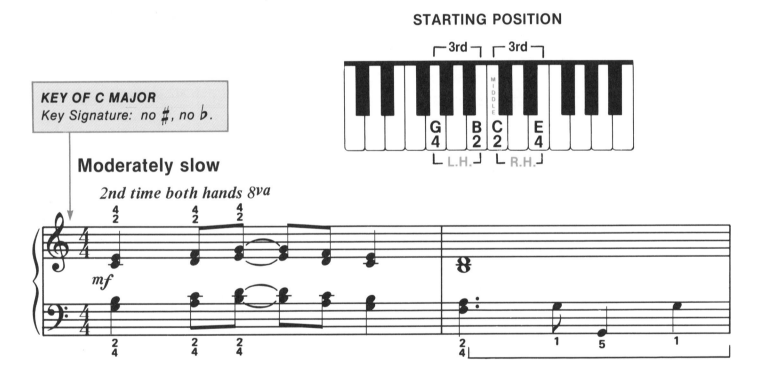

*This piece combines the use of the relative minor and major keys.

20

Calypso Rhumba

Use after GREENSLEEVES (page 30).

Andante moderato

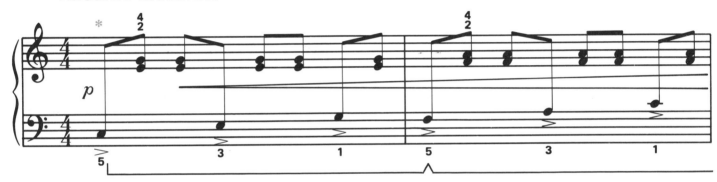

*Play eighth notes evenly!

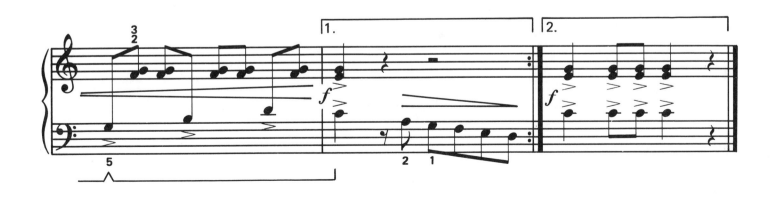

A Spooky Story

Use after GO DOWN MOSES (page 35).

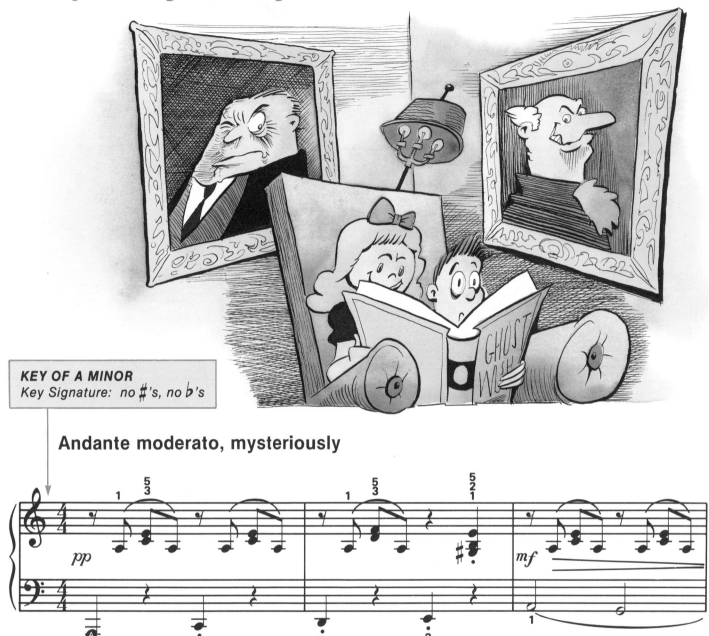

KEY OF A MINOR
Key Signature: no ♯'s, no ♭'s

Andante moderato, mysteriously

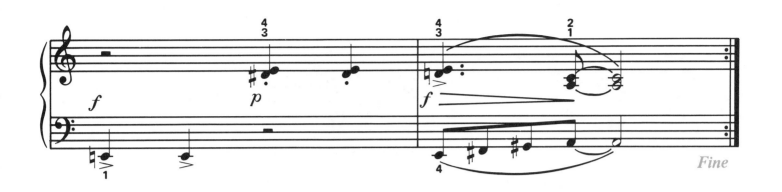

Fine

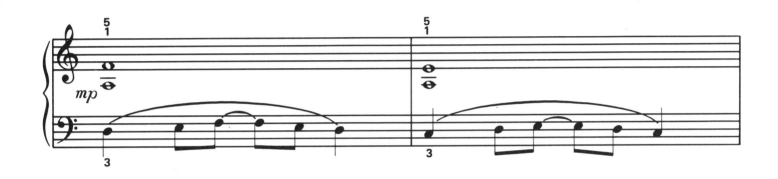

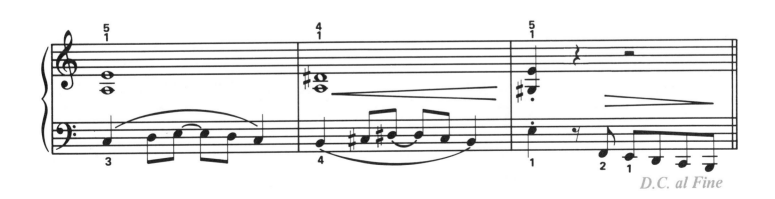

D.C. al Fine

Waltz in A Minor

Use after INTERMEZZO (page 36).

KEY OF A MINOR
Key Signature: no ♯'s, no ♭'s

Allegro moderato

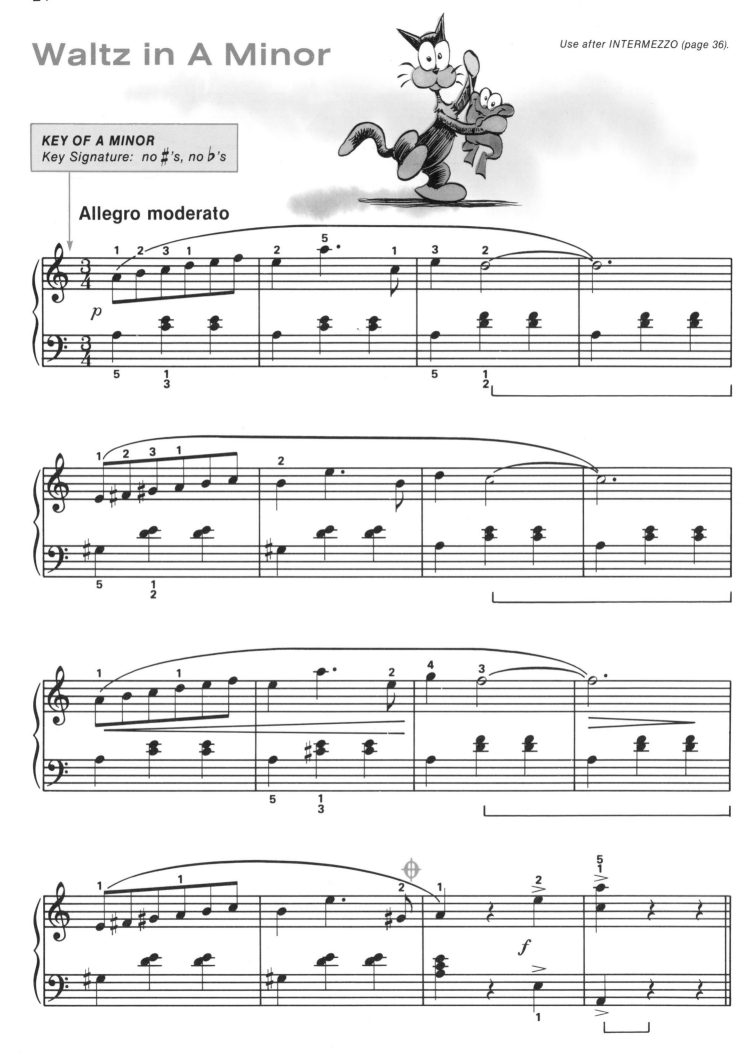

D.C. al 🕀, then CODA

Big Chief Yellow Hand

Use after SCARBOROUGH FAIR (page 39).

KEY OF D MINOR
Key Signature: 1 flat (B♭)

Moderato

Big Chief Yel - low Hand, the Chey-enne's great war-ri - or!

1. Come   and   call   your braves   to - geth-er   now!   Pow   Wow!
2. Sum - mon   all   your braves   to   gath-er   now!

Come,   Chey - enne!   And   build high   the   coun - cil   fires!

Speak, brave men! We must guard our te - pees!

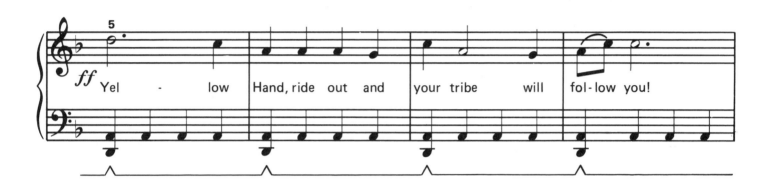

Yel - low Hand, ride out and your tribe will fol-low you!

Cross the prair -ie wide to join the Sioux! The Sioux!

Chey-enne and the Sioux!

Festive Dance

Use after RAISINS AND ALMONDS (page 40).

Allegro *

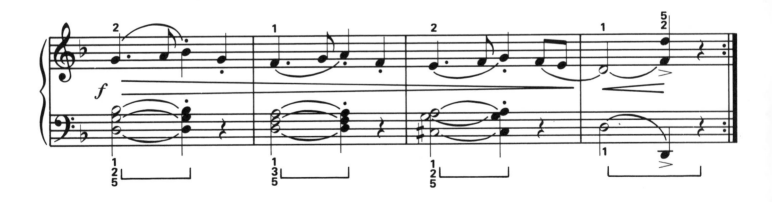

*It is also very effective to begin this piece very slowly and play gradually faster and faster to the end.

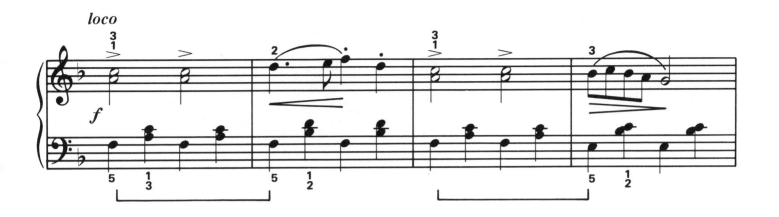

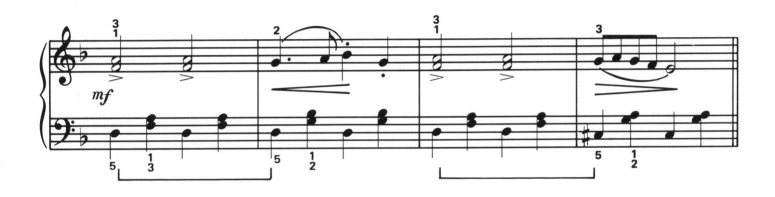

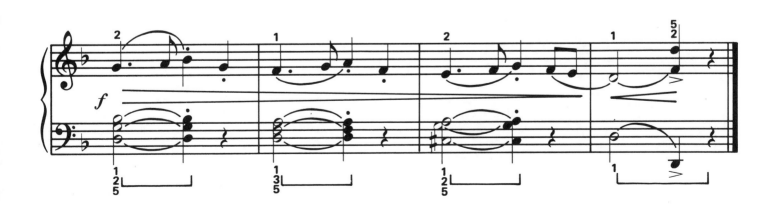

Concert Piece

Use after LA RASPA (page 44).

Allegro moderato

Both hands 8va -

With expression

mf *legato*

EXTENDED POSITION
(both hands)

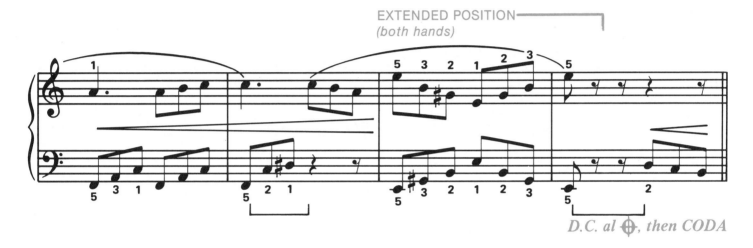

D.C. al ⊕, then CODA

⊕ Coda

Both hands *8va* -

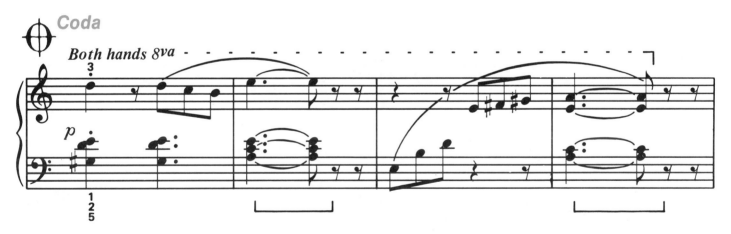

poco ritard.

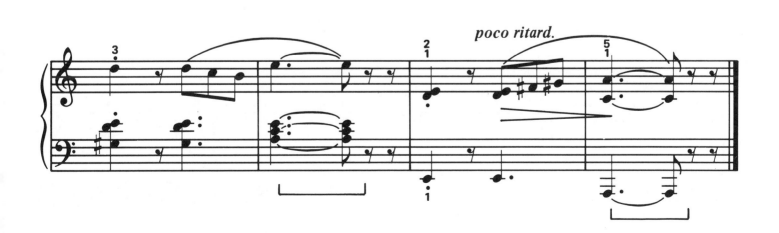

Pop! Goes the Weasel

Use after SCHERZO (page 46).